AN ANDERSON HOUSE BOOK

Off Broadway

Essays about the Theater

MAXWELL ANDERSON

WILLIAM SLOANE ASSOCIATES, INC.
Publishers *New York*

First printing

PRINTED IN THE UNITED STATES OF AMERICA

A slightly different version of the essay "Off Broadway" was delivered as a lecture at Rutgers University in 1942 as "The Basis of Artistic Creation in Literature" and was subsequently one of three essays published by the Rutgers University Press under the title *The Bases of Artistic Creation.* "Whatever Hope We Have" was the Founder's Day Address at Carnegie Institute in 1937. "Thoughts about the Critics" first appeared in the *New York Times* in February, 1947. "Poetry in the Theater" was the preface to *Winterset* when that play was brought out in book form. "The Essence of Tragedy" was written to be read at a session of The Modern Language Association in New York City, January, 1938. "Cut Is the Branch That Might Have Grown Full Straight" was read by Mr. Anderson at the Theater Convention and published in the *Authors' League Bulletin,* July, 1937. "The Politics of *Knickerbocker Holiday*" was the preface to that play when it appeared in book form. "The Uses of Poetry" was printed in *Stage* under the title "Yes, by the Eternal" as a rejoinder to an article by Max Eastman in the same magazine called "By the Eternal." "St. Bernard" was an address at a dinner in New York City in 1946 celebrating George Bernard Shaw's ninetieth birthday. "The Essence of Tragedy," "Whatever Hope We have," "Poetry in the Theater," and "The Uses of Poetry" were reprinted in *The Essence of Tragedy and Other Footnotes and Papers,* published in 1939 by Anderson House. Minor revisions have been made in several of these essays since their original appearance in print.

Off Broadway

Essays about the Theater

Contents

Off Broadway

Essays about the Theater

Thoughts About the Critics

SINCE EVEN APPROXIMATE JUSTICE IS HARD TO come by and absolute justice has never yet been reached anywhere, it is certainly too much to ask that a play receive just reviews the morning after it opens. In a world in which there are no final answers, in which every life, every nation, and every work of art must be judged and rejudged in successive years or generations as long as its influence endures, in which no professed solution of any problem—whether in the field of Socrates and Jesus or that of Newton and Einstein or that of Aeschylus and Shakespeare—will endure forever, it can hardly be hoped that an arbitrarily chosen group of newspapermen will arrive at their typewriters between eleven-thirty and midnight with the words about a new play that will satisfy anybody, even themselves.

* * *

The present tension between Manhattan critics and playwrights is due entirely to the enormous increase in the reviewers' power. A small group of the theater critics of New York have become, without intention but no less absolutely, a board of censors which a play must pass to achieve a run. And since New York is the only play-producing center for the country, these same critics constitute a censorship board for the theater of the United States. There was a time, not so long ago, when a play might, and often did, live down an adverse set of notices and find an audience, but the costs of production and operation are currently so high that this has become impossible. Plays now live or die by the verdict of the reviewers. It has come about that the reviewers' opinions are no longer the opinions of commentators but those of judges from whom there is no appeal. This court of final resort has the whole power of the metropolitan press behind it and operates in security, with no chance of adequate discussion or reply.

* * *

A new play in our theater is now a sitting duck. When the curtain goes up on it the critics are posted in a semicircle twenty or thirty feet away, armed with double-barreled shotguns and a supply of whatever food it is that makes ducks lay golden eggs. If they don't like the play they blast it off the stage. If they do like it they toss it their miraculous sustenance and it lives. What irritates the playwright about this situation is that critics can make mistakes. A critic has to decide in favor of the shotgun or the magic formula in time to catch the first edition. Naturally some good ducks die, some bad ducks live. And nobody really knows what's good or what's bad, in a duck or in a play. It's a matter of opinion, and it should be a matter of public opinion. Our system leaves the matter entirely to a few men who write for influential newspapers.

The newspapers, which are quite properly jealous of their own freedom, have set up and are conducting a censorship over the theater which is in absolute contradiction of the principles on which journalistic freedom is founded.

* * *

Every critic will maintain, of course, that he favors the fullest and freest operation of the theaters, without restriction on subject, treatment, or talent. Unfortunately, the censorship of which he is part does not function that way. Under the guise of a protection against incompetence it has set up and maintains a general control over theatrical production. Like all censorships, it degrades and diminishes the art it sets out to serve. Any group that stands between the public and an art form, dictating what the public may see, is a damaging force in a democracy.

* * *

The difference between power and influence is almost an absolute difference. The critics used to influence a play's destiny. Today they have the power of life and death over it. Plays are struck down on the opening night, or blown up on the opening night, with very brief consideration but complete finality. The public, reading tens of thousands of words of praise or dispraise, naturally attends or stays away as advised by the newspapers, and hits and failures are so arrived at.

* * *

The ability of the critics and the quality of their criticism are irrelevant to a discussion of censorship. A tyrant is a tyrant, beneficent or maleficent. But, obviously, critics do vary greatly in character and acumen, and their standards vary with the times. During a war all civilian standards are revised downward, and that's as true of playwriting and criticism as of everything else. The playwright finds himself confined to propaganda or escape. The critic becomes inured to poor stuff or leaves his desk in disgust. During the last war our theater experienced the usual dip in quality, accompanied by the usual rise in quantity. The best of the critics gave up and went into war work. Now that they are back on the job the critical appraisal of plays is both fairer and more imaginative. But this does not alter the fact that the critics have too much power—power which belongs rightfully in the hands of the public.

* * *

How and how much the uncensored judgment of the public would differ from that of the critics is a matter of opinion. My own observation makes me certain that the public would accept many more plays, many more playwrights, and a far wider range of subjects if it were allowed to choose for itself. It would be more tolerant of what is cheap, no doubt, and that would be a dubious gain, but it would also be more tolerant of what is serious. For the theater public contains audiences of many kinds, overlapping but almost infinite in variety. Left to themselves, these audiences would find out and support the plays that suited them, with the result that the theater would take in vastly more territory and reach both higher and lower than its present leading strings will allow.

* * *

When you start to consider the virtues and values of the critics you find a long list to their credit. As drumbeaters for something new or different or unexpectedly worth while they have often brought the public running to a theatrical venture which might have died unnoticed and unmourned. Sometimes one lonely enthusiast among them single-handed brings round the whole city and his fellow reviewers with it to recognition of a work that received mostly jeers and mutterings at its opening. Sometimes an unusually perceptive critic finds out and reassures a new talent, still doubtful of itself, but capable of more than it has dared to hope. A writer or actor never knows his own value, or whether he has any. He has to be told by somebody, has to see his reflection in another's eyes. As discoverers and champions the critics have often contributed substantially to theatrical growth. Sometimes an audience has sat doubtful and unbelieving before a new play, moved but unsure till the critics crystallized the emotion for them, gave them reasons for going along. Many a hung-fire first-night audience has caught and glowed and passed the word to future audiences because the critics caught on first and set the blaze. Then, as corrosive and abrasive elements, as removers of impurity, the critics have done white wings' service. They are as sensitive to a stale joke or to a rancid emotion as a gourmet to spoiled fish. Last, but not least, our critics are honest. They cannot be bought. Their opinions are their own, not dictated from above and not paid for. We have become so accustomed to honesty in our journalists that we overlook its rarity in this venal and increasingly totalitarian world. There are few countries left where newspaper opinion is neither official nor for sale.

* * *

When commentators become judges both their virtues and their vices are unduly magnified and some of their most engaging qualities become vices. A talent for derision, happy and laudable in a fellow in the bleachers, is out of place in an umpire. Enthusiasm in a judge has some of the quality of a court order spoken in anger. And though it is fitting that newspaper columnists and commentators be chosen for their readability, it is not fitting that judges, even judges of the arts, be so chosen. Most of the critics, and some of the most influential, though not all, were picked for their ability to hold and amuse their readers. Nothing amuses readers more than a public execution, with bloody details, and the temptation to gratify the populace with such exhibitions when you have been assigned the duties of judge, jury, and firing squad must be nearly irresistible.

* * *

And the largest section of the critics' circle speaks for one audience only. It represents a little group of theater-wise, picture-wise, café-society-wise people, who go to first nights as former generations of the elite went to church, to show themselves and their clothes and to be in on whatever is new. Also it is not always an advantage to a critic to be a graduate journalist, sharing the disillusions, the aversions, and the inevitable cynicism of that profession. But however they were chosen, however different their predilections, the critics all have one disadvantage in common—they all acquire, after a certain number of premières, the critics' occupational disease, an acute allergy to theatrical representation.

* * *

Very little has been written or said about the agony which critics suffer in the theater, but any experienced reviewer knows how real that agony is and how far it disables his judgment. His accustomed seat on the aisle becomes a dentist's chair to him, and he sits in it with the apprehension of one who has been drilled repeatedly to the quick. He suffers through acts and scenes only because he is paid to do it and because he takes a professional pride in the reports he writes of these sessions in hell. Nothing but novelty, or music, or fast-moving comedy, or torment greater than his own can take his mind off the routine of torture. He can give good reviews only to plays that distract him from his pain. Moreover, he has never chosen the play he is witnessing. He is the perpetual deadhead audience. He is there out of duty. If, with all this, he is ever capable of having a good time in the theater, it's in the nature of a small miracle. This was a minor matter when the critic was a commentator. If he remains a judge it will be fatal. The plays of a democratic society must be written for audiences, not for professional tasters of entertainment.

* * *

For our faith in democracy is a faith that the people choose best for themselves, that no overlord, specialist, committee, class, or group should decide what is good for the men and women of a nation. Furthermore, the arts of a democracy are its life. Business, law, politics, government, science—these are outward signs of what men are thinking, but the arts are the thoughts themselves. And of all the arts the theater can come closest to an affirmation of what we believe. You can say a part of it in a poem, a little of it in a song, a share of it in a novel or a painting, but the theater—or even the moving picture if the powers that control it were to lose their grip for a moment—can put man's faith in himself into exhilaration and worship and make a place for a nation in the world of time and space. Personally I don't trust any critic—or anybody else, including myself—to know when a play has said something worth listening to or worth saving. I do trust the public in a democracy. That's the only faith I have.

St. Bernard

BACK IN 1918 OR ABOUT THAT TIME I WROTE A one-paragraph review (that was all the magazine wanted) of *Heartbreak House* in which I said that Shaw was a brilliant writer but no playwright. That was before I'd written any plays, and I know now that I was quite wrong about Bernard Shaw and about *Heartbreak House.* Of course other people have been wrong before, and some very eminent people. El Greco once observed about Michelangelo (I quote this from an excellent essay by Lee Simonson on shifting aesthetic values), "He is a very good man and a good Italian but he simply cannot paint." Now my errors are not so important as El Greco's, and there may be some question as to how Shaw stacks up against Michelangelo, but otherwise there's a parallel in the remarks. We all have a hard time seeing the virtues of our contemporaries, especially if we're working on projects of our own, and with opposite convictions. In 1918 I put J. M.

Synge a great deal higher than Shaw in my pantheon. Later on I was inclined to set O'Casey higher than Shaw. But the older I get, the more plays I read and see, and the more I read in the volumes of St. Bernard, the more credit I give him. And now—finally, I think —I have changed my mind with a vengeance, for I set him at the head of all modern playwrights. He is a more considerable figure than Molière or Schiller or Chekhov or Strindberg or Ibsen, or any Irishman or American so far. He will loom larger with the passage of time.

This is an opinion, of course, and there's no proving one opinion more just than another. Also I'd better reserve the right to change my mind again. By the time I'm ninety myself (and it can happen to the most unlikely people) I may be rooting for somebody else. Also I must explain that I have made no critical study of Shaw's works. I have read him for pleasure only. Plays that are to endure must succeed not only on the stage but also in the library—and Shaw will bear a lot of reading and rereading. I have read and reread him. And I base my revised opinion on the fact that Shaw has illuminated a larger area of the modern intellectual landscape than anybody else. Reading or seeing his plays (to borrow a phrase) is like viewing our civilization by flashes of lightning.

Shaw is a very great man, a man with an enormously capacious and rapid brain, a brilliant stylist, a humanitarian, and—more or less in spite of himself—a great playwright. For he didn't set out to be a playwright at all. He didn't see that destiny before him at the beginning of his career. All the verbal magic and mental dexterity he found himself with as a youth in London he dedicated to reform. It was his intention—a rather sophomoric one which a lot of writers have by-passed—to make over the world. He took up a double armful of causes. Vegetarianism, anti-vivisection, socialism, anti-inoculationism, anti-this and anti-that, dress reform, speech reform, spelling reform, pro-this and pro-that. He was continually on the boxes of Hyde Park or the platforms of the societies which seemed to him to hold the keys to truth and the future. He became so ready on his feet, so quick at verbal riposte, so adept at turning his opponents' arguments against themselves, so nimble at extempore dialectic, that it was impossible for an antagonist to back him into a corner he couldn't slip out of, at the same time turning the laugh to his own advantage. Nobody in our time has been so lightning-fast with words and ideas, shooting from the hip and on the wing. Shaw lifted the art of debate to such levels of subtlety and insight that when by chance he came to write his first play he found that comedy was no heavy task for him. It was a mere matter of carrying on a glittering debate among imaginary characters. And he knew so well every emotional and logical position that could be taken by the human mind that his characters were no trouble to him, either. A character in a comedy is always a man or woman in an argument of some sort, and since there was no possible argument in which Shaw was not thoroughly at home, there was no possible comedy character or attitude that lay outside his range. And as his thought matured he discovered that tragedy was also a great debate and that he could create tragic characters.

I don't mean this as a belittling analysis. For Shaw didn't stop at the boundaries of dialectic. He pushed dialectic over into the realms of the spirit and considered every aspect of man and superman with a logic and a wit so flashing as often to seem superhuman. And as time went on he began to see that he could not change the world, that reform was not the answer—and then he went over to evolution and the Life Force as his hope for mankind. And when he began to have doubts that the Life Force could work fast enough to save us, he stepped across still another line into the kingdom of despair which Shakespeare and Sophocles had occupied before him. In his greatest plays—in *Saint Joan* and *Heartbreak House*—he has come out on the other side of hope and is with the great poets of all time, no longer a reformer, no longer a partisan—and, though a debater still, his debate is, in these plays, over the great problems of life and death, the eternal insoluble human dilemma.

The difference between comedy and tragedy seems to be this—the writer of comedy assumes that something can be done immediately to save men from themselves, and the writer of tragedy knows that there is no immediate way out. He knows that the burning questions of reform are all old, that men have sought the answers since the morning of history, and that the answers will not be found in his time, that nothing final will come of anything he does or says. Shaw began, as a young man, with a belief that all the ways to salvation were plain before humanity and only needed pointing out. He ends as a mystic who knows that we begin and end in mystery and that all faiths are delusions. His greatness is partly the result of his having lived a long time and learned mightily as he aged. Out of his stock of early certainties he has kept a few minor samples and habits—vegetarianism, for one—but he is aware that nothing can be defended because there is nothing he himself could not demolish. He has discovered that he can spin the spiderweb of belief in any direction over the abyss of doubt that is man's sole habitation. He has discovered that in a world where no man knows anything surely the man who assumes a conviction can be king.

But he has been honest. He has tried hard for absolutes. He has tried not to deceive himself or anyone else. And it follows that one by one he has taken up and defended, and one by one he has abandoned and destroyed, practically every position a man can take in seeking a faith for himself and for mankind. Like a swallow trapped indoors he has plunged against every window and found them all shut. The worth of his work lies in this—that in expounding, defending, attacking, and laying bare all the conceivable aspects of belief and all the possible motives for action he has irradiated almost the whole of a century with the unquenchable wildfire of an extraordinary brain. As far as thought can reach he has reached, and having done that he has taken in more territory than any other man whose life has been lived in his time.

Off Broadway

During the Second World War it seemed obvious that we were fighting to protect the earth and ourselves from men who believed that might makes right, that control of the sources of information makes truth, and that power makes justice. We believed violently enough to go to war about it that might is only sometimes right, that the sources of information should be at once open and uncontaminated, and that justice can only be arrived at by some kind of common consent which includes not only those to whom justice is to be applied but also those by whom it is carried out. When the war was over, the people of the democracies began to look hard and perhaps a little resentfully at these principles which had cost us so many billions, so many years, and so many lives. And for the first time in modern history it became apparent to us that we had emerged into an age of complete unfaith—an age in which everything by which we live is on trial and nothing is taken for granted.

It became apparent, too, that the fundamentals on which a civilization rests can never be proved. We take them for granted or we don't take them at all. But the fact that the necessity for our democracy has been questioned by men willing to give up their lives to make the challenge good has affected our thinking profoundly. Though the Nazis did not win they made us unsure of ourselves. And because we are a young nation, not much given to thought or to doubt, our present doubts rock us to the foundations of the republic. We are facing the ancient insoluble dilemma of mankind, but to us it is new and in the nature of a catastrophe. America has always been sure of itself. America unsure is almost another nation—a sleepwalking nation, feeling its way into the unknown.

This affects all of us—the businessman, the philosopher, the laborer, the investment banker, the boy and girl playing in the street. If you don't know what your work is for, or whether it can be justified, you know nothing about yourself or the meaning of your life—and your children are very soon aware that you don't know. The judges and the police and the school system very soon feel this uncertainty. The stores, the factories, the government bureaus, and the stock exchange all feel it. It slows them all down. It takes the edge off all effort and the imagination out of enterprise.

But the man most affected is the professional writer or artist. The professor of philosophy may state, and even feel, the question more urgently than the writer; on the other hand, he has no driving necessity for finding an immediately workable plan for living. He can talk the situation over with his students and take his time. But a practicing artist or a professional writer who uses ideas in his work is bound to conclude something, makeshift or profound, or shut up shop completely.

And a playwright, who must say something intelligible in every production, is driven more directly than any other writer or artist to make up his mind about his world or be silent until he can make up his mind. A man would be a fool who was certain that his vision of current events was the only right one, who believed that he had come upon the secret of the universe, or who thought he had penetrated, for certain, to the basis of things in literature or anywhere else. But if he is going to put plays on the stage he must have at least fragmentary convictions. Sometimes his convictions are subconscious; sometimes they are inherited. Sometimes the convictions that underlie the most modern and snappy of productions are simple-minded or old-fashioned. But dig for them and you will find them. A play can't be written without them—or, at least, it can't be a success—because no audience is satisfied with a play which doesn't take an attitude toward the world. Every artist is at a loss in a confused civilization, but the playwright is in the worst plight of all. For the best practice of his craft he needs a stable society within a stable congeries of nations. Our modern world has been the scene of vast mental and social confusion, and the theater has been shaken with every shift in the ideological weather. Those who have kept going as writers within it have done so because they could cling to inner beliefs not easily destroyed by exterior storm. Or because they believed in nothing and could simulate whatever belief happened to be popular.

Those who are old enough to remember the nineteen-twenties will recall one curious fallacy of that decade, a belief more extraordinary than the prosperity that accompanied it. The victory over Germany and the efflorescence of invention that went with and followed the war, staggered men's minds. They saw the earth and its creatures in a bright new scientific light in which the customs of our ancestors appeared to be based on inexplicable and ridiculous taboos. Religion was not only questioned but put aside. Social codes were scrutinized under microscopes, and scrapped along with the rules of Leviticus. There was a general belief that men were done with the foolishness of wars and conquest as a method of settling differences. On this side of the Atlantic at least, we thought men had learned better than to try again to grasp the steering wheel of the earth by violence. We closed our eyes to smoking volcanoes of malignity, wondering how men would adjust themselves to a life in which there was no more hell-fire. We believed that the war had been a mistake, that no war was worth fighting, even for the victor; that Gandhi was right, that non-resistance was more powerful than force, that the conqueror destroyed himself automatically, that good and evil came in unavoidable waves, that good would inevitably turn into evil and evil into good with the passage of years. We rejected the war between good and evil. We would fight it no more. Villains, we said, are made villains by circumstances, and we must fight the circumstances, not the poor individual wretches whose anti-social actions caused trouble. Peace conferences were held and humane agreements concerning the usages of war were made among the nations. Naval strength was adjusted by treaty, and battleships were sunk to limit the power of those who had too much. It was an era of reason and good feeling that seemed destined to last interminably. Having emerged into sunlight out of the darkness of history, we saw our way clearly. We saw clearly in those high-minded times that the race was not going to live by the Old or the New Testament. It was going to live in the light of scientific day, making its choices freely among the fruits of the new trees of knowledge. Crime was a disease, and curable. Poverty was a disease, and curable. God was to be replaced by a sort of higher expedience, arrived at by laboratory methods. There was no sin except that which made for inefficiency. Honor was a holdover from the past, retained mainly for business reasons. The need for sexual restraint was abolished by the discovery of contraceptives. Men were like trees, the race was like a forest. They needed nothing except proper conditions and free functioning to grow and prosper as never before. If there had been scarcities, if men had lacked and suffered, all lacks could be supplied by the multiplication of machinery. If there had been grim and terrible feuds over the love of a woman, the ownership of land or the conflicts of worship, they had become laughably unnecessary. Love should be free, land should bear beyond the capacity of the race to consume, religion was a laid ghost. We were to go forward and eat and drink and be merry, and right and wrong would dissolve into a series of realistic choices between that which was healthful and that which was poisonous.

Since every man's thinking is directed or deflected by that of his age, we all of us, in the nineteen-twenties, stared hard at this new and dazzling age which we were assured was just beyond the next elections. To most people it was not only acceptable but welcome as an inevitable step forward. What kind of environment it would make for us if it came none of us knew. What dangers lurked under its shiny blessings we could only guess. There was no precedent for the utopia of invention. Men were mainly concerned, then as always, with the problem of keeping some kind of place for themselves, philosophically and economically, on this whirling ball. It was no longer expected that the gods would help us. We knew no gods and honored no decalogue.

Yet it was in these godless nineteen-twenties that I stumbled upon the only religion I have. And I came upon it in the most unlikely and supposedly godless of places. I was a journalist, and I knew nothing about the theater except casually from the outside. But I wrote a verse tragedy, being bored with writing editorials, and a gallant producer put it on the stage—for no reason that I can see now. It failed quietly, as it deserved, but after its production the theater tugged at me, its rewards dazzled me—and I wrote other plays, some of them successful. However, from the very beginning the theater was to me, in some fundamental ways, an exasperating puzzle. Some plays succeeded, some did not, and why, nobody knew. Success on the stage seemed to be one of the ultimate mysteries. Leaving aside the questions of acting and directing, the problems of theme, story, and writing appeared only more confused when discussed by the professors of playwriting. I developed a theory which still looks cogent to me—that a playwright's first success was always largely accidental. After that he could analyze what he had done, and begin to develop an intuition that would take him through the maze of difficulties and dangers his action and dialogues must thread. But intuition is an unreliable guide, and I was not as intuitive as some others. I needed a compass—or a pole star—or some theory of what the theater was about, and I had none.

However, I did discover that there were rules of playwriting which could not be broken. One by one I unearthed them for myself, or dug them out of the treatises of predecessors. And by and by some of them began to look like essentials. Let me cite a few of the first that came clear to me.

1. The story of a play must be the story of what happens within the mind or heart of a man or woman.

It cannot deal primarily with external events. The external events are only symbolic of what goes on within.

2. The story of a play must be a conflict, and specifically, a conflict between the forces of good and evil within a single person. The good and evil to be defined, of course, as the audience wants to see them.

3. The protagonist of a play must represent the forces of good and must win, or, if he has been evil, must yield to the forces of the good, and know himself defeated.

4. The protagonist of a play cannot be a perfect person. If he were he could not improve, and he must come out at the end of the play a more admirable human being than he went in.

When I had once begun to make discoveries of this sort, they came thick and fast. And they applied not, as is natural to suppose, to extraordinary plays only—to Shakespeare and Jonson and the Greeks—but to all plays, and to those in our modern repertory as much as any others. I add a few more of the ancient and inescapable rules as they came to me.

5. The protagonist of a play must be an exceptional person. He or she cannot be run-of-the-mill. The man in the street simply will not do as the hero of a play. If a man be picked from the street to occupy the center of your stage, he must be so presented as to epitomize qualities which the audience can admire. Or he must indicate how admirable human qualities can be wasted

or perverted—must define an ideal by falling short of it, or become symbolic of a whole class of men who are blocked by circumstances from achieving excellence in their lives.

6. Excellence on the stage is always moral excellence. A struggle on the part of a hero to better his material circumstances is of no interest in a play unless his character is somehow tried in the fire, and unless he comes out of his trial a better man.

7. The moral atmosphere of a play must be healthy. An audience will not endure the triumph of evil on the stage.

8. There are human qualities for which the race has a special liking on the stage: in a man, positive character, strength of conviction not shaken by opposition; in a woman, fidelity, passionate faith. There are qualities which are especially disliked on the stage: in a man, cowardice, any refusal to fight for a belief; in a woman, an inclination toward the Cressid.

These are precepts, of course, only for the writing of a play. The presentation is quite as important, and hedged about with as many commandments; but since I am neither actor nor director I am aware of only a few. Let me indicate what some of them are. When you choose an actor to play the leading role in a play you try to find a man who is not only a good actor, but who can be looked upon with admiration by the people out in front. This may seem simple enough to do, but it is not. When you are casting a play you become acutely conscious of the mental, physical and moral shortcomings of the human race. If you will stand in the lobby of a theater as the patrons come in and examine them with the idea of finding a man or a woman who could take a leading part in the play, you will be disconcerted by the imperfection of mankind. So few, so lamentably few, would stand the test of the center of the stage, the concentrated lights and the concentrated scrutiny of a thousand fellow creatures insistent on perfection, or an approach to perfection. In that pool of light at the center of the stage all defects are magnified. Pick out the handsome, the attractive, the beautiful, the youthfully engaging and let the dissecting stares play on them one by one. Suppose you have chosen the best out of thousands. Suppose they are all attractive at first glance; but look again, for the audience will look again. Perhaps you find a too heavy jaw, slightly thin nostrils, an inadequate forehead, a shifty eye, faintly clumsy legs, an awkward pose, overeagerness, timidity, a slight indication of grossness, illness, hesitant speech. Physical defects are less disastrous than mental or spiritual faults. One in ten thousand will be worthy to stand in that blaze, and like as not that one, even if he be an actor, is a bad one, tied up emotionally, unable to pour his soul into words and emotional states not his own.

I list these technical difficulties because they began eventually to have one meaning for me. They mean that the purpose of the theater is to find, and hold up to our regard, what is admirable in the human race.

The theatrical profession may protest as much as it likes, the theologians may protest, and the majority of those who see our plays would probably be amazed to hear it, but the theater is a religious institution devoted entirely to the exaltation of the spirit of man. It has no formal religion. It is a church without a creed, but there is no doubt in my mind that our theater, instead of being, as the evangelical ministers used to believe, the gateway to hell, is as much a worship as the theater of the Greeks, and has exactly the same meaning in our lives.

When I first wrote plays this statement would have seemed incredible to me. Broadway in the twenties, in the thirties, and now in the forties, has always worn an air of hard, garish, cheap professionalism. The lights, the chilly box-office men, the ornate and dirty buildings, the groups of actors lingering in drugstores and along side streets, these all proclaim clearly a place of entertainment for sale. The priest and priestesses of these temples are certainly unaware of the nature of their profession. But consider what they sell, and you face a different prospect. The plays that please most and run longest in these dusty alleys are representative of human loyalty, courage, love that purges the soul, grief that ennobles. Sometimes a simple tale like *Victoria Regina,* the story of a young girl faced suddenly with the responsibilities of an empire, unequal at first to the task, but developing and learning with the years, acquiring tolerance, wisdom and dignity, dying a great queen. Perhaps the story of Abraham Lincoln, a man with great endowments but afraid of life, forcing himself to face life, forcing himself to lead a nation in a war that sickened his soul, emerging at the end a great man. For those to whom this theory is novel, it will seem easy to refute. The case of *Rain* will come up, where the uncritical tolerance and good will of a prostitute are held better moral guides than the fanatical zeal of the missionary. They are better moral guides, no doubt of it. But the play does not praise the woman for being a prostitute. It finds virtue in her despite her vocation. It does not condemn the man for his religion, but for the perversion of religion into an evil force. The case of *Tobacco Road* will come up, in which a poor white family struggles with a burden of poverty, ignorance, and adverse social conditions. There is no doubt that the run of the play was stimulated by a morbid curiosity concerning the unashamed sexual customs of the inhabitants of that mythical road through the tobacco fields, but if there had been no moral values in the piece nobody would have cared to see it. The sexual customs or lack of them wouldn't have drawn a nickel. There were heroic qualities in Jeeter Lester and his strange brood. They lacked many virtues. They were shiftless, dishonest, financially hopeless. But they were not afraid. They faced existence as it was handed out to them in a way that made them both pathetic and tragic. Nothing better is expected of any hero on the stage than this—that he take up what arms he has against what enemies assail him and come out of the battle with his morale intact. Jeeter Lester kept very little except his self-respect, but he did keep that, and those who saw him had a respect both for him and for the human spirit that cannot be quenched by squalor. I have witnessed several plays on Broadway that attempted to imitate *Tobacco Road* by duplicating the adverse conditions and the resultant twisted lives and depressed morals. But they were failures because they assumed that the public wanted only dirt. It wasn't the dirt of *Tobacco Road* that gave it a long run, but the accompanying, and to many invisible, gallantry of its people.

Perhaps I have made my point nauseatingly clear, but I should like to present a little more evidence. As everybody knows, the great plays of the world—those accepted by civilization as part of a great heritage and played for centuries—these are almost all concerned with the conduct of exceptional men or women in positions of great responsibility, men with tragic faults and weaknesses but with mind and strength enough to overcome, in the struggle with evil forces, both those within themselves and those without. This is *Hamlet, The Cid, Prometheus.* And it is also, please note, *Abe Lincoln in Illinois.* In such cases it is obvious that some kind of religious ritual is involved in reviving these symbols of national or cultural faith in a public performance. The *Oresteia* of Aeschylus is a ritual of crime and punishment, and ends by stating that Zeus himself must grow and learn and change if he is to avoid injustice. But here again we have a modern instance. *The Green Pastures* treats exactly the same theme, God's justice, and ends with exactly the same lesson, that God must learn and grow and change or his rigid justice will become an injustice in the end. I am fairly certain that Marc Connelly did not intentionally preach from the text of Aeschylus, but his play is no less a religious observance because it was presented in a plush-chaired theater off our own gaudy Broadway. The worshipers pay a fairly high rent for their pews in the theatrical Forties, and not many of them realize that they are assisting in a worship, but they sit in church nevertheless, and acquire virtue thereby according to their understanding and the wisdom and skill of the functioning playwright. *Oedipus Tyrannus* and *Macbeth* and *Little Eyolf* and *The Little Foxes* teach one and all that an evil action revenges itself upon the doer. *Antigone* and *Hamlet* and ten thousand modern plays argue that injustice is a corrosive, and will eat the heart out of him who practices it. Analyze any play you please which has survived the test of continued favor, and you will find a moral or a rule of social conduct or a rule of thumb which the race has considered valuable enough to learn and pass along. Take such seemingly meaningless escapades as *You Can't Take It with You* and *The Time of Your Life.* The first says simply that money isn't everything, and the second says, as plainly as the author can speak, that tolerance is the great virtue. These are platitudes, of course. A play is not required to make ethical discoveries. It is only required to have a meaning, and a sound one—one, that is, which is accepted as sound by its audience. Put on a play which sets out to prove that dishonesty is the best policy and vice is triumphant in human affairs, and the audience will refuse it coldly. They don't want to believe it and they won't. You can poke farcical fun at homicide, as in *Arsenic and Old Lace* or *The Playboy of the Western World* or *The Beggar's Opera,* but you cannot seriously praise an unrepentant murderer. The race —or the audiences—will not allow it. They will register disapproval and they will stay away.

There have been critics who held that the theater was central among the arts because it is a synthesis of all of them. Now I confess that the theater appears to me to be the central art—but for a different reason. It does bring together all the arts, or a number of them. But its distinction is that it brings them together in a communal religious service. Any other art, practiced separately, can be either moral or amoral, religious or pagan, affirmative or despairing. But when they come together in the theater they must affirm, they cannot deny. It is as if poetry, music, narration, dancing, and the mimetic arts were bits and pieces of theatrical art, stripped away to function alone and rudderless without the moral compulsion of the theater.

And now I must give a definition of what seems to me morally sound. If morality depends on the existence of good and evil, then the good and evil of the theater are those acceptable to the present audience. The mores of the Greek theater are not at all points consistent with ours, though they come close to them. If good and evil alter, the playwright must go along. To some artists the present good may seem evil and the present evil good. That has happened often in the case of a poet or a prophet. A playwright cannot run so far ahead of his audience, for he must find a common denominator of belief in his own generation, and even the greatest, the loftiest, must say something which his age can understand. The heart of the theater is a belief in democracy, a belief that the people must make their own standards, must decide for themselves what to worship.

In brief, I have found my religion in the theater, where I least expected to find it, and where few will credit that it exists. But it is there, and any man among you who tries to write plays will find himself serving it, if only because he can succeed in no other way. He will discover, if he works through his apprenticeship, that the theater is the central artistic symbol of the struggle of good and evil within men. Its teaching is that the struggle is eternal and unremitting, that the forces which tend to drag men down are always present, always ready to attack, that the forces which make for good cannot sleep through a night without danger. It denies the doctrine of the nineteen-twenties emphatically. It denies that good and evil are obverse and reverse of the same coin, denies that good can win by waiting. It denies that wars are useless and that honor is without meaning. It denies that we can live by the laboratory and without virtue. It affirms that the good and evil in man are the good and evil of evolution, that men have within themselves the beasts from which they emerge and the god toward which they climb. It affirms that evil is what takes man back toward the beast, that good is what urges him up toward the god. It affirms that these struggles of the spirit are enacted in the historic struggles of men—some representing evil, some good. It offers us criteria for deciding what is good and what is evil. Set a man on the stage and you know instantly where he stands morally with the race. Set Hitler on the stage and loathing will rise from every seat in the house. Even in Germany, had he been a character in a play, he would have been hated and despised. You cannot be pitiless, merciless, ruthless, arrogant, and without tolerance on the stage, and be considered a hero. That which is considered despicable on the stage will be held despicable in real life—not only evil but those who will not fight evil are rejected on both sides of the footlights. A man who accepts the wave of the future and analyzes honor to a breath can be the comedian to be laughed at but he cannot be the protagonist. According to the worshipers of the good who sit in our theaters a hero may have his doubts and indecisions, for that's only human, but when it comes to the test he must be willing to take steel in his bosom or take lead through his intestines or he resigns his position as a man. The audiences, sitting in our theaters, make these rules and, in setting them, define the purposes and beliefs of homo sapiens. There is no comparable test that I know of for what is good in the human soul, what is most likely to lead to that distant and secret destination which the race has chosen for itself and will somehow find.

Whatever Hope We Have

THERE IS ALWAYS SOMETHING SLIGHTLY EMbarrassing about the public statements of writers and artists, for they should be able to say whatever they have to say in their work, and let it go at that. Moreover, the writer or artist who brings a message of any importance to his generation will find it impossible to reduce that message to a bald statement, or even a clearly scientific statement, because the things an artist has to communicate can be said only in symbols, in the symbols of his art. The work of art is a hieroglyph, and the artist's endeavor is to set forth his vision of the world in a series of picture writings which convey meanings beyond the scope of direct statement. There is reason for believing that there is no other way of communicating new concepts save the artist's way, no other way save the artist's way of illuminating new pathways in the mind. Even the mathematician leaves the solid plane of the multiplication table and treads precariously among symbols when he advances toward ideas previously unattained.

But I am not reaching for such ideas at the moment. I am writing this for the young people of this country who may at this moment be trying to decide what to do with their lives. Shall it be business, politics, law, science, or any of the subheads under these? Shall it be something that vaguely comes under the label of "the arts," and which our civilization only in rare cases encourages? Shall it be the army, the navy, the university? Shall it be exploration or invention? I am not unprejudiced in this matter and I wish to state a case.

Let me begin then with a picture of the earth as I see it. The human race, some two billion strong, finds itself embarked on a curious voyage among the stars, riding a planet which must have set out from somewhere and must be going somewhere, but which was cut adrift so long ago that its origin is a matter of speculation and its future beyond prophecy. Our planet is of limited area, and our race is divided into rival nations and cultures that grow and press on one another, fighting for space and the products of the ground. We are ruled by men like ourselves, men of limited intelligence, with no foreknowledge of what is to come, and hampered by the constant necessity of maintaining themselves in power by placating our immediate selfish demands. There have been men among us from time to time who had more wisdom than the majority, and who laid down precepts for the conduct of a man's brief life. Some of them claimed inspiration from beyond our earth, from spirits or forces which we cannot apprehend with our five senses. Some of them speak of gods that govern our destinies, but no one of them has had proof of his inspiration or of the existence of a god. Nevertheless there have been wise men among them, and we have taken their precepts to heart and taken their gods and their inspiration for granted.

Each man and woman among us, with a short and harried life to live, must decide for himself what attitude he will take toward the shifting patterns of government, justice, religion, business, morals, and personal conduct. We are hampered as well as helped in these decisions by every prejudice of ancestry and race, but no man's life is ready-made for him. Whether he chooses to conform or not to conform, every man's religion is his own, every man's politics is his own, every man's vice or virtue is his own, for he alone makes decisions for himself. Every other freedom in this world is restricted, but the individual mind is free according to its strength and desire. The mind has no master save the master it chooses.

And each must make his choices, now as always, without sufficient knowledge and without sufficient wisdom, without certainty of our origin, without certainty of what undiscovered forces lie beyond known scientific data, without certainty of the meaning of life, if it has a meaning, and without an inkling of our racial destiny. In matters of daily and yearly living, we have a few, often fallible, rules of thumb to guide us, but on all larger questions the darkness and silence about us is complete.

Or almost complete. Complete save for an occasional prophetic voice, an occasional gleam of scientific light, an occasional extraordinary action which may make us doubt that we are utterly alone and completely futile in this incomprehensible journey among the constellations. From the beginning of our story men have insisted, despite the darkness and silence about them, that they had a destiny to fulfill—that they were part of a gigantic scheme which was understood somewhere, though they themselves might never understand it. There are no proofs of this. There are only indications—in the idealism of children and young men, in the sayings of such teachers as Christ and Buddha, in the vision of the world we glimpse in the hieroglyphics of the masters of the great arts, and in the discoveries of pure science, itself an art, as it pushes away the veils of fact to reveal new powers, new laws, new mysteries, new goals for the eternal dream. The dream of the race is that it may make itself better and wiser than it is, and every great philosopher or artist who has ever appeared among us has turned his face away from what man is toward whatever seems to him most godlike that man may become. Whether the steps proposed are immediate or distant, whether he speaks in the simple parables of the New Testament or the complex musical symbols of Bach and Beethoven, the message is always to the effect that men are not essentially as they are but as they imagine and as they wish to be. The geologists and anthropologists, working hand in hand, tracing our ancestry to a humble little animal with a rudimentary forebrain which grew with use and need, reinforce the constant faith of prophet and artist. We need more intelligence and more sensitivity if ever an animal needed anything. Without them we are caught in a trap of selfish interest, international butchery, and a creed of survival that periodically sacrifices the best to the worst, and the only way out that I can see is a race with a better brain and superior inner control. The artist's faith is simply a faith in the human race and its gradual acquisition of wisdom.

Now it is always possible that he is mistaken or deluded in what he believes about his race, but I myself accept his creed as my own. I make my spiritual code out of my limited knowledge of great music, great poetry, and great plastic and graphic arts, including with these, not above them, such wisdom as the Sermon on the Mount and the last chapter of Ecclesiastes. The test of a man's inspiration for me is not whether he spoke from a temple or the stage of a theater, from a martyr's fire or a garden in Hampstead. The test of a message is its continuing effect on the minds of men over a period of generations. The world we live in is given meaning and dignity, is made an endurable habitation, by the great spirits who have preceded us and set down their records of nobility or torture or defeat in blazons and symbols which we can understand. I accept these not only as prophecy, but as direct motivation toward some far goal of racial aspiration. He who meditates with Plato, or finds himself shaken by Lear's "fivefold never" over Cordelia, or climbs the steep and tragic stairway of symphonic music, is certain to be better, both intellectually and morally, for the experience. The nobler a man's interests the better citizen he is. And if you ask me to define nobility, I can answer only by opposites, that it is not buying and selling, or betting on the races. It might be symbolized by such a figure as a farmer boy in western Pennsylvania plowing corn through a long afternoon and saying over and over to himself certain musical passages out of Marlowe's *Doctor Faustus.* He might plow his corn none too well, he might be full of what we used to call original sin, but he carries in his brain a catalytic agent the presence of which fosters ripening and growth. It may be an impetus that will advance him or his sons an infinitesimal step along the interminable ascent.

The ascent, if we do climb, is so slow, so gradual, so broken, that we can see little or no evidence of it between the age of Homer and our own time. The evidence we have consists in a few mountain peaks of achievement, the age of Pericles, the centuries of Dante and Michelangelo, the reign of Elizabeth in England, the century and a half of music in Germany, peaks and highlands from which the masters seem to have looked forward into the distance far beyond our plodding progress. Between these heights lie long valleys of mediocrity and desolation, and, artistically at least, we appear to be miles beneath the upper levels traversed behind us. It must be our hope as a nation that either in pure art or in pure science we may arrive at our own peak of achievement, and earn a place in human history by making one more climb above the clouds.

The individual, the nation, and the race are all involved together in this effort. Even in our disillusioned era, when fixed stars of belief fall from our sky like a rain of meteors, we find that men cling to what central verities they can rescue or manufacture, because without a core of belief neither man nor nation has courage to go on. This is no figure of speech, no sanctimonious adjuration—it is a practical, demonstrable fact which all men realize as they add to their years. We must have a personal, a national, and a racial faith, or we are dry bones in a death valley, waiting for the word that will bring us life. Mere rationalism is mere death. Mere scientific advance without purpose is an advance toward the waterless mirage and the cosmic scavengers. The doctrine of Machiavelli is a fatal disease to the citizen or the state. The national conscience is the sum of personal conscience, the national culture the sum of personal culture—and the lack of conscience is an invitation to destruction, the lack of culture an assurance that we shall not even be remembered.

No doubt I shall be accused of talking a cloudy philosophy, of mixed metaphors and fantasy, but unless I misread my history, the artist has usually been wiser even about immediate aims than the materialist or the enthusiast for sweeping political reform. The artist is aware that man is not perfect, but that he seeks perfection. The materialist sees that men are not perfect, and erects his philosophy on their desire for selfish advantage. He fails quickly always, because men refuse to live by bread alone. The utopian sees that men seek perfection and sets out to achieve it or legislate it into existence. He fails because he cannot build an unselfish state out of selfish citizens, and he who asks the impossible gets nothing. The concepts of truth and justice are variables approaching an imaginary limit which we shall never see; nevertheless, those who have lost their belief in truth and justice and no longer try for them are traitors to the race, traitors to themselves, advocates of the dust.

To my mind a love of truth and justice is bound up in men with a belief in their destiny; and the belief in their destiny is of one piece with national and international culture. The glimpse of the godlike in man occasionally vouchsafed in a work of art or prophecy is the vital spark in a world that would otherwise stand stock-still or slip backward down the grade, devoid of motive power.

For national growth and unity the artist's vision is the essential lodestone without which there is no coherence. A nation is not a nation until it has a culture which deserves and receives affection and reverence from the people themselves. Our culture in this country has been largely borrowed or sectional or local; what we need now to draw us together and make us a nation is a flowering of the national arts, a flowering of the old forms in this new soil, a renaissance of our own. If we want to live, or deserve to live, as a force or in history, we must somehow encourage the artists who appear among us, and we must encourage excellence among them. How to go about it is a problem entirely unsolved. I wish I could believe that prizes, or critics, or governmental endowments were effective stimulants toward effort or excellence in any artistic field. They may be occasionally, but the greatest achievements have occurred in the absence of endowments, or professional critics or prizes, seemingly as the result of a feverish desire for accomplishment in any single art, permeating a whole society during a period long enough to allow for more than one generation of devotees. Probably an artist can ask nothing better than a free society which likes his work and is willing to pay for it.

Looking ahead, I have no more than a hope that our nation will sometime take as great a place in the cultural history of the world as has been taken by Greece or Italy or England. So far we have, perhaps, hardly justified even the hope. But what hope there is for us lies in our nascent arts, for if we are to be remembered as more than a mass of people who lived and fought wars and died, it is for our arts that we will be remembered. The captains and the kings depart; the great fortunes wither, leaving no trace; inherited morals dissipate as rapidly as inherited wealth; the multitudes blow away like locusts; the records and barriers go down. The rulers, too, are forgotten unless they have had the forethought to surround themselves with singers and makers, poets and artificers in things of the mind.

This is not immortality, of course. So far as I know there is no immortality. But the arts make the longest reach toward permanence, create the most enduring monuments, project the farthest, widest, deepest influence of which human prescience and effort are capable. The Greek religion is gone, but Aeschylus remains. Catholicism shrinks back toward the papal state, but the best of medieval art perishes only where its pigments were perishable. The Lutheranism of Bach retains little content for us, but his music is indispensable. And there is only one condition that makes possible a Bach, an Aeschylus, or a Michelangelo—it is a national interest in and an enthusiasm for the art he practices. The supreme artist is only the apex of a pyramid; the pyramid itself must be built of artists and art-lovers, apprentices and craftsmen so deeply imbued with a love for the art they follow or practice that it has become for them a means of communication with whatever has been found highest and most admirable in the human spirit. To the young people of this country I wish to say: if you practice an art, be proud of it, and make it proud of you; if you now hesitate on the threshold of your maturity, wondering what rewards you should seek, wondering perhaps whether there are any rewards beyond the opportunity to feed and sleep and breed, turn to the art which has moved you most readily, take what part in it you can, as participant, spectator, secret practitioner, or hanger-on and waiter at the door. Make your living any way you can, but neglect no sacrifice at your chosen altar. It may break your heart, it may drive you half mad, it may betray you into unrealizable ambitions or blind you to mercantile opportunities with its wandering fires. But it will fill your heart before it breaks it; it will make you a person in your own right; it will open the temple doors to you and enable you to walk with those who have come nearest among men to what men may sometime be. If the time arrives when our young men and women lose their extravagant faith in the dollar and turn to the arts, we may then become a great nation, nurturing great artists of our own, proud of our own culture and unified by that culture into a civilization worthy of our unique place on this rich and lucky continent—and worth remembering, perhaps, when our wealth and our luck run out.

Poetry in the Theater

EXPERIMENT IN THE THEATER IS MADE DIFFICULT and expensive by the fact that a play must find an audience at once or have no chance of finding one later. There is no instance in the theater of a writer who left behind him a body of unappreciated work which slowly found its public, as, for example, the work of Shelley and Keats found a belated public after they had left the scene. It follows that the playwright must pluck from the air about him a fable which will be of immediate interest to his time and hour, and relate it in a fashion acceptable to his neighbors. That is the job for which he is paid. But he will also try to make that fable coincide with something in himself that he wants to put in words. A certain cleverness in striking a compromise between the world about him and the world within has characterized the work of the greatest as well as the least of successful playwrights, for they must all take an audience with them if they are to continue to function. Some may consider it blasphemy to state that this compromise must be a considered and conscious act—will believe that the writer should look in his heart and write—but in the theater such an attitude leaves the achievement entirely to chance, and a purely chance achievement is not an artistic one.

Yet when a writer sits down before white paper to make this necessary compromise he finds himself alone among imponderables. Nobody has ever known definitely what any audience wanted. A choice must be made with only intuition and a mass of usually irrelevant information as the guides. One who thinks more of his job than his fame will therefore play safe by repressing his personal preferences and going all the way in the direction of what he believes the public wants. One who thinks as much of his fame as of his job will often hope the public is ready for a theme only because he wishes to treat it—or ready for a dramatic method only because he wishes to employ it.

I may have been somewhat guilty of this last misapprehension in *Winterset,* for I have a strong and chronic hope that the theater of this country will outgrow the phase of journalistic social comment and reach occasionally into the upper air of poetic tragedy. I believe with Goethe that dramatic poetry is man's greatest achievement on his earth so far, and I believe with the early Bernard Shaw that the theater is essentially a cathedral of the spirit, devoted to the exaltation of men, and boasting an apostolic succession of inspired high priests which extends further into the past than the Christian line founded by St. Peter. It has been, even at its best, a democratic temple, decorated with more gargoyles than saints, generously open to wits, clowns, excoriating satirists, false prophets, and crowds of money-changers with a heavy investment in the mysteries. Lately it has recognized the mysteries only as a sideshow, and has been overrun with guides who prove to an eager public that all saints are plaster and all prophets fakes.

When Shaw began his furious critical assault on the romantic theater which was lingering out the last decade of the nineteenth century he became the prophet of the theater of realistic social protest which he has dominated in England during his lifetime and which is still the controlling pattern for plays of the English-speaking stage. A few original and outstanding playwrights, J. M. Synge, Sean O'Casey and Eugene O'Neill among them, may seem to fall completely outside the Shavian category. Synge was too poetic, symbolic, and savage to work in any social harness, O'Casey's world-searing irony is too tremendous to come under the head of protest, and O'Neill has been seeking an escape from realism throughout his whole career. All three went beyond Shaw's amusing balance and clarity into a tragic, sinister, and often brutal world. Synge wrote of that world with extraordinary beauty and a lethal precision; O'Casey and O'Neill write of it with passion and a sometimes choking defiance. O'Casey, in addition, has a power over words which lifts such a play as *The Plough and the Stars* out of its local setting. That play gave me an exhilarating experience in the theater. Nothing on the stage ever moved me more until the arrival of Olivier in the Yeats version of *Oedipus.*

None of the prose moderns, not Synge, not O'Casey, not O'Neill, not Shaw himself, has written anything which we can set unquestioningly beside *Oedipus the King* or *Macbeth* or many others we can pick up in the library—and the reason for that is a fairly simple one. Our modern dramatists are not poets, and the best prose in the world is inferior on the stage to the best poetry. It is the fashion, I know, to say that poetry is a matter of content and emotion, not of form, but this is said in an age of prose by prose writers who have not studied the effect of form on content or who wish to believe there is no limit to the scope of the form they have mastered. To me it is inescapable that prose is the language of information and poetry the language of emotion. Prose can be stretched to carry emotion, and in some exceptional cases, as in Synge's and O'Casey's plays, can occasionally rise to poetic heights by substituting the unfamiliar speech rhythms of an untutored people for the rhythm of verse. But under the strain of an emotion the ordinary prose of our stage breaks down into inarticulateness, just as it does in life. Hence the cult of understatement, hence the realistic drama in which the climax is reached in an eloquent gesture or a moment of meaningful silence.

The majority of present-day playgoers have never

seen any other kind of play and see no reason why there should be any other. So emphatic is this feeling that one is doubtful of being able to explain to this majority that verse was once the accepted convention on the stage, as prose is now, that prose fought its way into the playbooks with difficulty at the beginning of the scientific era in which we live and will hold its place there only so long as men make a religion of fact and believe that information, conveyed in statistical language, can make them free.

For the stage is still a cathedral, but just now a journalistic one, dominated by those who wish to offer something immediate about our political, social, or economic life. Like every other existing condition it gives the illusion of permanence, but it will change. An age of reason will be followed once more by an age of faith in things unseen. The cathedral will then house the mysteries again, along with the jugglers and the vendors of rose-colored spectacles. What faith men will then have, when they have lost their certainty of salvation through laboratory work, I don't know, having myself only a faith that men will have a faith. But that it will involve a desire for poetry after our starvation diet of prose I have no doubt. Men have not been altered by the invention of airplanes and the radio. They are still alone and frightened, holding their chance tenure of life in utter isolation in this desolate region of revolving fires. Science may answer a few necessary questions for them, but in the end science itself is obliged to say that the fact is created by the spirit, not spirit by the fact. Our leading scientists are already coming to this conclusion, rather reluctantly and with some surprise.

Unless I am greatly mistaken many members of the theater audience have anticipated this conclusion by one of those intuitional shortcuts which confound the devotees of pure reason, and are not only ready but impatient for plays which will take up again the consideration of man's place and destiny in prophetic rather than prosaic terms. It is incumbent on the dramatist to be a poet, and incumbent on the poet to be prophet, dreamer, and interpreter of the racial dream. Men have come a long way from the salt water in the millions of years that lie behind them, and have a long way to go in the millions of years that lie ahead. We shall not always be as we are, but what we are to become depends on what we dream and desire. The theater, more than any other art, has the power to weld and determine what the race dreams into what the race will become. All this may sound rather farfetched in the face of our present Broadway, and Broadway may laugh at it unconscionably, but Broadway is itself as transient as the real-estate values under its feet. Those of us who fail to outlive the street in which we work will fail because we have accepted its valuations and measured our product by them.

For though on the surface we are still a pioneer people, ashamed of aspiration, offended by the deliberate quest for beauty, able to accept beauty only when it seems achieved by accident, our pioneer days are over and we must set about molding ourselves at least one art form worthy of the leading nation of the world or be set down finally as barbarians and carry that name with us into the darkness to which all nations sooner or later descend. Our theater is the one really living American art. It has size, vitality, and popular interest. But it is still in the awkward and self-conscious age, concealing its dreams by clowning, burlesquing the things it most admires. Those who have read their literary history carefully know that now is the time for our native amusements to be transformed into a national art of power and beauty. It needs the touch of a great poet to make the transformation, a poet comparable to Aeschylus in Greece or Marlowe in England. Without at least one such we shall never have a great theater in this country, and he must come soon, for these chances don't endure forever.

I must add, lest I be misunderstood, that I have not mistaken myself for this impending phenomenon. I have made my living as teacher, journalist, and playwright, and have only that skill as a poet which may come from long practice of an art I have loved and studied and cannot let alone. When I wrote my first play, *White Desert,* I wrote it in verse because I was weary of plays in prose that never lifted from the ground. It failed, and I did not come back to verse again until I had discovered that poetic tragedy had never been successfully written about its own place and time. There is not one tragedy by Aeschylus, Sophocles, Euripides, Shakespeare, Corneille, or Racine which did not have the advantage of a setting either far away or long ago. With this admonition in mind I wrote *Elizabeth the Queen* and a succession of historical plays in verse, some of them successful, and found myself immediately labeled a historical and romantic playwright, two terms I found equally distasteful. *Winterset* is largely in verse, and treats a contemporary tragic theme, which makes it more of an experiment than I could wish, for the great masters themselves never tried to make tragic poetry out of the stuff of their own times. To do so is to attempt to establish a new convention, one that may prove impossible of acceptance, but to which I was driven by the lively historical sense of our day—a knowledge of period, costume, and manners which almost shuts off the writer on historical themes from contemporary comment. Whether or not I have solved the problem in *Winterset* is probably of little moment. But it must be solved if we are to have a great theater in America. Our theater has not yet produced anything worthy to endure —and endurance, though it may be a fallible test, is the only test of excellence.

The Essence of Tragedy

ANYBODY WHO DARES TO DISCUSS THE MAKING OF tragedy lays himself open to critical assault and general barrage, for the theorists have been hunting for the essence of tragedy since Aristotle without entire success. There is no doubt that playwrights have occasionally written tragedy successfully, from Aeschylus on, and there is no doubt that Aristotle came very close to a definition of what tragedy is in his famous passage on catharsis. But why the performance of tragedy should have a cleansing effect on the audience, why an audience is willing to listen to tragedy, why tragedy has a place in the education of men, has never, to my knowledge, been convincingly stated. I must begin by saying that I have not solved the Sphinx's riddle which fifty generations of skillful brains have left in shadow. But I have one suggestion which I think might lead to a solution if it were put to laboratory tests by those who know something about philosophical analysis and dialectic.

There seems no way to get at this suggestion except through a reference to my own adventures in playwriting, so I ask your tolerance while I use myself as an instance. A man who has written successful plays is usually supposed to know something about the theory of playwriting, and perhaps he usually does. In my own case, however, I must confess that I came into the theater unexpectedly, without preparation, and stayed in it because I had a certain amount of rather accidental success. It was not until after I had fumbled my way through a good many successes and an appalling number of failures that I began to doubt the sufficiency of dramatic instinct and to wonder whether or not there were general laws governing dramatic structure which so poor a head for theory as my own might grasp and use. I had read the *Poetics* long before I tried playwriting, and I had looked doubtfully into a few well-known handbooks on dramatic structure, but the maxims and theories propounded always drifted by me in a luminous haze—brilliant, true, profound in context, yet quite without meaning for me when I considered the plan for a play or tried to clarify an emotion in dialogue. So far as I could make out every play was a new problem, and the old rules were inapplicable. There were so many rules, so many landmarks, so many pitfalls, so many essential reckonings, that it seemed impossible to find your way through the jungle except by plunging ahead, trusting to your sense of direction and keeping your wits about you as you went.

But as the seasons went by and my failures fell as regularly as the leaves in autumn I began to search again among the theorists of the past for a word of wisdom that might take some of the gamble out of playwriting. What I needed most of all, I felt, was a working definition of what a play is, or perhaps a formula which would include all the elements necessary to a play structure. A play is almost always, probably, an attempt to recapture a vision for the stage. But when you are working in the theater it's most unsatisfactory to follow the gleam without a compass, quite risky to trust "the light that never was on sea or land" without making sure beforehand that you are not being led straight into a slough of despond. In other words you must make a choice among visions, and you must check your chosen vision carefully before assuming that it will make a play. But by what rules, what maps, what fields of reference can you check so intangible a substance as a revelation, a dream, an inspiration, or any similar nudge from the subconscious mind?

I shan't trouble you with the details of my search for a criterion, partly because I can't remember it in detail. But I reread Aristotle's *Poetics* in the light of some bitter experience, and one of his observations led me to a comparison of ancient and modern playwriting methods. In discussing construction he made a point of the recognition scene as essential to tragedy. The recognition scene, as Aristotle isolated it in the tragedies of the Greeks, was generally an artificial device, a central scene in which the leading character saw through a disguise, recognized as a friend or as an enemy, perhaps as a lover or a member of his own family, some person whose identity had been hidden. Iphigeneia, for example, acting as priestess in an alien country, receives a victim for sacrifice and then recognizes her own brother in this victim. There is an instant and profound emotional reaction, instantly her direction in the play is altered. But occasionally, in the greatest of the plays, the recognition turned on a situation far more convincing, though no less contrived. Oedipus, hunting savagely for the criminal who has brought the plague upon Thebes, discovers that he is himself that criminal—and since this is a discovery that affects not only the physical well-being and happiness of the hero, but the whole structure of his life, the effect on him and on the direction of the story is incalculably greater than could result from the more superficial revelation made to Iphigeneia.

Now scenes of exactly this sort are rare in the modern drama except in detective stories adapted for the stage. But when I probed a little more deeply into the memorable pieces of Shakespeare's theater and our own I began to see that though modern recognition scenes are subtler and harder to find, they are none the less present in the plays we choose to remember. They seldom have to do with anything so naïve as disguise or the unveiling of a personal identity. But the element of discovery is just as important as ever. For the mainspring in the mechanism of a modern play is almost invariably a discovery by the hero of some element in his environment or in his own soul of which he has not been aware—or which he has not taken sufficiently into account. Moreover, nearly every teacher of playwriting has had some inkling of this, though it was not until after I had worked out my own theory that what they said on this point took on accurate meaning for me. I still think that the rule which I formulated for my own guidance is more concise than any other, and so I give it here: A play should lead up to and away from a central crisis, and this crisis should consist in a discovery by the leading character which has an indelible effect on his thought and emotion and completely alters his course of action. The leading character, let me say again, must make the discovery; it must affect him emotionally; and it must alter his direction in the play.

Try that formula on any play you think worthy of study, and you will find that, with few exceptions, it follows this pattern or some variation of this pattern. The turning point of *The Green Pastures,* for example, is the discovery by God, who is the leading character, that a God who is to endure must conform to the laws of change. The turning point of *Hamlet* is Hamlet's discovery, in the play scene, that his uncle was unquestionably the murderer of his father. In *Abe Lincoln in Illinois* Lincoln's discovery is that he has been a coward, that he has stayed out of the fight for the Union because he was afraid. In each case, you will note, the discovery has a profound emotional effect on the hero, and gives an entirely new direction to his action in the play.

I'm not writing a disquisition on playwriting and wouldn't be competent to write one, but I do want to make a point of the superlative usefulness of this one touchstone for play structure. When a man sets out to write a play his first problem is his subject and the possibilities of that subject as a story to be projected from the stage. His choice of subject matter is his personal problem, and one that takes its answer from his personal relation to his times. But if he wants to know a possible play subject when he finds it, if he wants to know how to mold the subject into play form after he has found it, I doubt that he'll ever discover another standard as satisfactory as the modern version of Aristotle which I have suggested. If the plot he has in mind does not contain a playable episode in which the hero or heroine makes an emotional discovery, a discovery that practically dictates the end of the story, then such an episode must be inserted—and if no place can be found for it the subject is almost certainly a poor one for the theater. If this emotional discovery is contained in the story, but is not central, then it must be made central, and the whole action must revolve around it. In a three-act play it should fall near the end of the second act, though it may be delayed till the last; in a five-act play it will usually be found near the end of the third, though here also it can be delayed. Everything else in the play should be subordinated to this one episode—should lead up to or away from it.

Now this prime rule has a corollary which is just as important as the rule itself. The hero who is to make the central discovery in a play must not be a perfect man. He must have some variation of what Aristotle calls a tragic fault; and the reason he must have it is that when he makes his discovery he must change both in himself and in his action—and he must change for the better. The fault can be a very simple one—a mere unawareness, for example—but if he has no fault he cannot change for the better, but only for the worse, and for a reason which I shall discuss later, it is necessary that he must become more admirable, and not less so, at the end of the play. In other words, a hero must pass though an experience which opens his eyes to an error of his own. He must learn through suffering. In a tragedy he suffers death itself as a consequence of his fault or his attempt to correct it, but before he dies he has become a nobler person because of his recognition of his fault and the consequent alteration of his course of action. In a serious play which does not end in death he suffers a lesser punishment, but the pattern remains the same. In both forms he has a fault to begin with, he discovers that fault during the course of the action, and he does what he can to rectify it at the end. In *The Green Pastures* God's fault was that he believed himself perfect. He discovered that he was not perfect, that he had been in error and must make amends. Hamlet's fault was that he could not make up his mind to act. He offers many excuses for his indecision until he discovers that there is no real reason for hesitation and that he has delayed out of cowardice. Lincoln, in *Abe Lincoln in Illinois,* has exactly the same difficulty. In the climactic scene it is revealed to him that he had hesitated to take sides through fear of the consequences to himself, and he then chooses to go ahead without regard for what may be in store for him. From the point of view of the playwright, then, the essence of a tragedy, or even of a serious play, is the spiritual awakening, or regeneration, of his hero.

When a playwright attempts to reverse the formula, when his hero makes a discovery which has an evil effect, or one which the audience interprets as evil, on his character, the play is inevitably a failure on the stage. In *Troilus and Cressida* Troilus discovers that Cressida is a light woman. He draws from her defection the inference that all women are faithless—that faith in woman is the possession of fools. As a consequence he turns away from life and seeks death in a cause as empty as the love he has given up, the cause of the strumpet Helen. All the glory of Shakespeare's verse cannot rescue the play for an audience, and save in *Macbeth* Shakespeare nowhere wrote so richly, so wisely, or with such a flow of brilliant metaphor.

For the audience will always insist that the alteration in the hero be for the better—or for what it believes to be the better. As audiences change the standards of good and evil change, though slowly and unpredictably, and the meanings of plays change with the centuries. One thing only is certain: that an audience watching a play will go along with it only when the leading character responds in the end to what it considers a higher moral impulse than moved him at the beginning of the story, though the audience will of course define morality as it pleases and in the terms of its own day. It may be that there is no absolute up or down in this world, but the race believes that there is, and will not hear of any denial.

And now at last I come to the point toward which I've been struggling so laboriously. Why does the audience come to the theater to look on while an imaginary hero is put to an imaginary trial and comes out of it with credit to the race and to himself? It was this question that prompted my essay, and unless I've been led astray by my own predilections there is a very possible answer in the rules for playwriting which I have just cited. The theater originated in two complementary religious ceremonies, one celebrating the animal in man and one celebrating the god. Old Greek Comedy was dedicated to the spirits of lust and riot and earth, spirits which are certainly necessary to the health and continuance of the race. Greek tragedy was dedicated to man's aspiration, to his kinship with the gods, to his unending, blind attempt to lift himself above his lusts and his pure animalism into a world where there are other values than pleasure and survival. However unaware of it we may be, our theater has followed the Greek patterns with no change in essence, from Aristophanes and Euripides to our own day. Our more ribald musical comedies are simply our approximation of the Bacchic rites of Old

Comedy. In the rest of our theater we sometimes follow Sophocles, whose tragedy is always an exaltation of the human spirit, sometimes Euripides, whose tragicomedy follows the same pattern of an excellence achieved through suffering. The forms of both tragedy and comedy have changed a good deal in nonessentials, but in essentials—and especially in the core of meaning which they must have for audiences—they are in the main the same religious rites which grew up around the altars of Attica long ago.

It is for this reason that when you write for the theater you must choose between your version of a phallic revel and your vision of what mankind may or should become. Your vision may be faulty, or shallow, or sentimental, but it must conform to some aspiration in the audience, or the audience will reject it. Old Comedy, the celebration of the animal in us, still has a place in our theater, as it had in Athens, but here, as there, that part of the theater which celebrated man's virtue and his regeneration in hours of crisis is accepted as having the more important function. Our comedy is largely the Greek New Comedy, which grew out of Euripides' tragicomedy, and is separated from tragedy only in that it presents a happier scene and puts its protagonist through an ordeal which is less than lethal.

And since our plays, aside from those which are basically Old Comedy, are exaltations of the human spirit, since that is what an audience expects when it comes to the theater, the playwright gradually discovers, as he puts plays before audiences, that he must follow the ancient Aristotelian rule: he must build his plot around a scene wherein his hero discovers some mortal frailty or stupidity in himself and faces life armed with a new wisdom. He must so arrange his story that it will prove to the audience that men pass through suffering purified, that, animal though we are, despicable though we are in many ways, there is in us all some divine, incalculable fire that urges us to be better than we are.

It could be argued that what the audience demands of a hero is only conformity to race morality, to the code which seems to the spectators most likely to make for race survival. In many cases, especially in comedy, and obviously in the comedy of Molière, this is true. But in the majority of ancient and modern plays it seems to me that what the audience wants to believe is that men have a desire to break the molds of earth which encase them and claim a kinship with a higher morality than that which hems them in. The rebellion of Antigone, who breaks the laws of men through adherence to a higher law of affection, the rebellion of Prometheus, who breaks the law of the gods to bring fire to men, the rebellion of God in *The Green Pastures* against the rigid doctrine of the Old Testament, the rebellion of Tony in *They Knew What They Wanted* against the convention that called on him to repudiate his cuckold child, the rebellion of Liliom against the heavenly law which asked him to betray his own integrity and make a hypocrisy of his affection, even the repudiation of the old forms and the affirmation of new by the heroes of Ibsen and Shaw, these are all instances to me of the groping of men toward an excellence dimly apprehended, seldom possible of definition. They are evidence to me that the theater at its best is a religious affirmation, an age-old rite restating and reassuring man's belief in his own destiny and his ultimate hope. The theater is much older than the doctrine of evolution, but its one faith, asseverated again and again for every age and every year, is a faith in evolution, in the reaching and the climb of men toward distant goals, glimpsed but never seen, perhaps never achieved, or achieved only to be passed impatiently on the way to a more distant horizon.

"Cut Is the Branch That Might Have Grown Full Straight"

THIS LAST DRAMATIC SEASON HAS SEEN ALMOST as many revivals as original plays—a sure sign that the theater is slowing down creatively—and a good many moving-picture enthusiasts hang about the side streets where playhouses are to be torn down, waiting to follow the corpse of the Broadway theater to its last resting place. I think they were ill advised to purchase those flowers and mourning vestments so soon. The theater is not so healthy as it was in 1927, not so great an industry as it was in 1937, but it will still outlive and outlast the cinema. The theater is the phoenix of the arts. It has died many deaths in many cities and many languages—and come to life again, sometimes in the same cities and languages, sometimes in other languages and in cities across the sea. There is no doubt that the moving pictures have sucked most of the current lifeblood out of Broadway, and that the anemia of the last few

New York seasons was largely caused by the draining off of promising writers and actors into Hollywood, but that does not mean that Hollywood has acquired durability and that the theater will die. Hollywood will die because the seeds of its death were planted in its invention, and a lethal gene lurked in that camera eye from the beginning. The theater will live because it can be re-created at any time by the proverbial actor with a passion to enunciate and four planks to stand on, but the pictures will die because they are a mechanical invention and will inevitably be superseded.

A lot of young writers who have been trapped, driven, and lured into giving up playwriting for picture writing are the real losers in this situation. No writer of a picture will ever be remembered as such. A playwright has a chance to say something memorable. The lucky few who have managed to stay with the theater, or have escaped young from the studios, will never get rich and they will have to live by their wits, but they belong to themselves and they will be allowed to say what they think as long as they manage to interest an audience. As for the picture writers who might have been playwrights, the appropriate epitaph for them is from *Dr. Faustus:*

Cut is the branch that might have grown full straight,
And burnéd is Apollo's laurel bough.

It's not a new thing for playwrights to have to live by their wits. The theater has lived by its wits during most of its history. It will continue to live by its wits and to be the most important American art so long as the censors let it alone, so long as it is not so rich as to become fatheaded, and so long as it numbers a little corps of competent actors and playwrights who love it. If it were possible to kill the theater, or even to injure it vitally, while these essentials are left intact, it would be dead now. It carries more parasites, survives more negligence, bleeds inwardly from more fratricidal warfare than any going concern in the history of the world. I've seldom heard of anybody trying to help the theater. I've heard of the government planning to tax it more, of the real estate operators gouging it, of the scalpers scalping it, of the state loading the building and licensing laws against it, of the unions holding it up, of the dramatists quarreling with producers, of the moving pictures devouring its children, writers and actors, as fast as they appear, and still our theater is the center of civilization in New York and in the United States, and quite amazingly the foremost theater in the world.

And I think I know why. The theater is a democratic art, a democracy of the mind. Nothing counts in it except what gifts you have and what you can do with them. It doesn't help to be rich in the theater. You can't buy success. It doesn't matter if you're poor. If you have what it takes, you can carve success out of thin air with a shoehorn. Nobody's too good for the theater. Go as high as you can, no matter who you are, and the audience is a little ahead of you, hoping you'll go higher next time. Nobody's too bad for the theater.

Be as low as the law allows, and, if you're clever about it, if you know how to make filth amusing, the audience is still ahead of you, hoping you'll go lower next time. But high or low, if you haven't gauged the public taste correctly, you've lost your labor and you're on the street again, probably minus your shoestrings. Time after time you gamble your brains and lose. Only once in a while you gamble and win. This incredible and exhilarating state of anarchy obtains nowhere else. It annoys some people on the outside, and they try to put a stop to it. It drives a lot of people on the inside to drink, to the sanitarium, or into that haven of rest, the moving pictures.

Now when a man really wants to quit the theater for the pictures there should be no effort to stop him. Maybe he hasn't the stomach for our God-given, magical witches' brew. Maybe he isn't up to swimming the waters of chaos. Maybe he prefers security to freedom. If he does, the pictures will be a great relief to him. Hollywood is just the opposite of the stage. It is safe, sane, stodgy, organized, methodical, businesslike, and regulated. Hollywood's work is all teamwork. Nobody succeeds alone or fails alone in that rainless picnic ground. Only by unhappy accident, immediately rectified by those in charge, does one man ever put his stuff on the screen undoctored to suit studio specifications. It follows that everybody has an alibi, nobody is blamed for anything, nobody is ever fired, and the pictures are practically all Hollywood soup out of the same kettle, only the country has to swallow them anyway under the poisonous block-booking system.

If you are a playwright and go to Hollywood, you discover that there are no authors in moving pictures. There are no authors because the picture companies own all the copyrights and are registered in Washington as the writers of the scripts turned out by the hired hands on the lot. They can change what you write and they will. After you've written your damnedest, they'll set seven more galley slaves to work on it, singly and in groups, and by the time the product is ready for consumption it will taste like all the rest of the soup in all the other cans labeled with the trade-mark of your studio. A playwright on Broadway fails far oftener than he succeeds, but he's nobody's hired man. What he has written is his own and may be changed only with his consent. It happens that a work of art is always one man's concept, carried out in so far as possible without deviation from the dream that went into its making. In New York a play can be, sometimes is, a projection in the round of one man's imaginative vision. It follows that the theater can foster and present a work of art, that the excellence of our art of the theater is limited only by the endowment of those of us who work in it, and that we should be wary of the kind of gilt-edged, assured success that Hollywood experiences. Our anarchy, our failures, our freedom, and our achievement go hand in hand.

But quite apart from the question of artistic freedom in pictures, there are many of us who would always prefer the stage while it continued to yield any kind of meager living, for the theater has been and will continue to be a great form, an art that has bred many masters and will cradle many more before our civilization loses its taste for dramatic expression. The pictures have no such past and can look forward to no such future. They came in as a mechanical invention, they will go out when that invention is excelled, as it will be. Some of you will consider this notion old-fashioned, no doubt, but wait a few years. While the boom is on nobody believes in the collapse. The good old moving pictures are not overlong for this world. And when they are gone they will be forgotten. They are too ephemeral in time and materials to create an art. Their artistic triumphs appear to me not so much exaggerated as mythical. The test of an art is endurance, and in any endurance contest the films have as much chance against the stage as the celluloid cat chasing the asbestos rat through hell. They have a wide audience now because they are cheap, and the cheaper product triumphs in the market. But they originate no arresting ideas, formulate no concepts, tell no story that hasn't been told before. They are a simulacrum of the real thing, a reprint series, a line of glossy, refurbished secondhand clothes. They are good enough, no doubt, for those who like them, but I have no respect for any man's judgment who gives them a place with the theater or above it.

Even if the studios did have an art form by the tail, the way the business is organized it would effectually shut off artistic effort. Suppose there were two or three gigantic companies in Manhattan that bought up all the actors and dramatists and set them to work concocting plays to order. Suppose these same companies owned legitimate theaters in every village and city and ordered all plays written to fit the nationwide common denominator. The companies would probably make money, the actors and dramatists would be sure of their pay checks, and a lot of people would be happier. But the theater as we know it would come to an end, would become as unimportant as the pictures are now, as vapid as an unsigned editorial. Let us not be too envious of the financial rewards and the tight organization of Hollywood. They are purchased at the price of regimentation—regimentation of the public through block booking and block advertising, regimentation of the artist by divesting him of his copyrights. High salaries in the paradise of the west are the mess of pottage for which the independent artists who work in Hollywood must sell their birthright.

Compromise and Keeping the Faith

ONE OF THE FIRST THINGS A PLAYWRIGHT learns in the theater is that a produced play is a compromise, and must be a compromise, between the original script and the acting and directing talent available. This should be pretty obvious, no doubt, but its application is difficult, nerve-racking, and a new, unexpected series of problems with every play. No actor ever fits any part exactly. No director ever sees a play exactly as the author imagined it. To illustrate the process of adjustment (though this is one of the simpler dilemmas) you may have to choose as your leading man, or lady, one of three who have these divergent advantages: one of them fits the part perfectly but is only a mediocre performer, a second is a brilliant actor but does not fit the part at all and will pull it out of shape, a third is not much of an actor but has an enormous Hollywood draw at the box office. No doubt you are fortunate to have

three to choose among—but usually the choice has to be made while somebody is waiting on the other end of a wire, and after a sleepless night over rewriting problems. Moreover, something like this same choice has to be made in regard to every actor in the play and in regard to nearly every line of the script. Usually you are pretty sure you could have been wrong —but the choices have to be made, they have to be made offhand, and they can't be erased. In the theater nobody is ever forgiven for an error. If there were such a thing as a perfect play—there isn't, of course—it would arrive on stage imperfect because of what it has to go through to get there. As some compensation for this state of things, plays sometimes arrive on stage more impressive than they are in manuscript or in print. It follows that directors and actors choosing plays have to make the same kind of compromise that playwrights make choosing directors, actors, themes, and words.

It may seem to the casual observer in the theater that nothing is sacred, that nothing is too good, or too near the heart of the project, to be thrown away if expediency requires. And that's where not only casual observers and newcomers, but also many old hands, go wrong. A play that's any good has an essential integrity which must not be sacrificed. What that integrity is, when it's endangered by current decisions, where it will bear reconsideration, and to what extent: these are questions that must be answered on the spur of the moment by the playwright and producer

—and answered correctly—or the play will fail. A play that doesn't have an essential integrity, and hasn't kept it throughout the million and one decisions of revision, casting, and rehearsals, isn't wanted by any public, and will be refused. Almost always, of course, that central essential soul is supplied by the playwright in the writing, and must be defended by the playwright throughout the storms and confusions of getting ready for an audience. At any rate, if that central living soul of the machine has not been saved intact, then the whole investment of brains, money, time, and talent has been useless.

To put these statements as nearly as possible in the shape of mathematical postulates:

1. Unless you and your play have a dream—or a conviction (much the same thing)—and unless you can defend that conviction against death and hell and the wiles of experienced tricksters, your play isn't worth producing.

2. Unless you are willing to make nearly every possible business and artistic concession to the play-producing setup, you'll probably never get your play on at all.

3. But if you let these concessions touch and injure the dream (or conviction) that animates your play (and those you deal with will try their damnedest to get at it) it isn't worth while putting on your play at all.

Every man is inclined to exaggerate the significance of his own job in the world, and no doubt I have looked at playwriting so long that I see in it a microcosm of all men's problems. But when I look out over the earth between bouts with plays I find a reproduction of the playwright's problems in every human effort.

Suppose you are a statesman or popular leader, trying to take a nation with you through a crisis in its destiny. Your first essential is a conviction about what must be done. The second essential is a willingness to bargain with every cheap local politician you need to get your measures through. Lincoln bargained in such fashion, and so did the second Roosevelt. But if in your bargaining you forget your convictions and sacrifice the thing you were trying to attain, then you become a run-of-the-mill politician yourself; your work is worth nothing, and the world will forget you gladly.

Suppose you edit or own a newspaper. To keep going every newspaper has to print all kinds of things that don't come near whatever journalistic ideals you have. You are the judge, you and your fellow editors, of how far you can go toward trash and still retain your self-respect. But cross that line, wherever it is, lose faith in your standards and go over to the mere dispensing of thrills and gossip, and from there on it doesn't matter what you decide or what your paper prints. It may make money for a while, but it will be despised and forgotten as rapidly as possible.

Suppose you are a lover of pure mathematics. You

get your highest pleasure out of solving abstruse problems that touch only the world of number and have no relation to human life or the tangible and visible universe. If you stick to such speculations your work is worthless to the world of men and probably—except as an amusement—to yourself. As soon as you begin to mingle observed and counted values into your mathematics their significance is suddenly enhanced. Without Michelson's experiment, Einstein's pure mathematics would never have hit on relativity. But the mathematics of the grocery store won't get you anything either, except possibly groceries.

Suppose you are a philosopher who has meditated long on human destiny and has arrived at a faith in what men must do to be saved. When you first begin to expound this faith—it may be to a trial audience of one—you will discover that certain adjustments are necessary to make it presentable and palatable. You make the adjustments—perhaps instinctively and extempore, perhaps after thinking the whole thing over. But if the faith itself is injured in the readjusting, then it would be better never to peddle that faith to your fellow men, for it no longer has validity, even for you.

Suppose you are a student of mental illnesses, and you have hit on a new treatment for certain psychological difficulties that promises to be effective in a large proportion of cases. But to perfect your treatment and round out your knowledge of its possibilities you have to work in a mental hospital where the methods and conditions sicken you to the heart. As an employee it is your duty to follow routines and apply therapeutic measures that you are convinced will damage and not help the patients. Should you remain with the hospital in order to gain the experience necessary to the elaboration of your theory, or should you leave rather than add to the darkness of the unfortunates you attend? This is a harder choice than most of the others, but in its essence it is the same question. How much will I adjust to the practical conditions of the world in order to gain ground for my faith?

Suppose you are a musician, a pianist who loves to play Bach and nobody else. Suppose you come to a period in your career when you could win both name and influence by broadening your programs and playing the works of other masters. Eventually that might mean that you could choose your programs and take the works of Bach to a vastly wider audience. Should you cling to your strict faith and your rigid Bach schedule, or should you include other musical prophets in your repertory? As with all these decisions, the responsibility sits squarely on your shoulders. You must decide, and take—for the rest of your life—the praise or the blame. And for eternity too, perhaps; for once in a while a man like Pythagoras or Socrates has a decision to make that influences the culture of a whole series of civilizations—so many that we can't see the end of them, and may regard the impulse as eternal so far as men are concerned.

Back in the theater we may be fairly sure that no

decision of ours will cast so long a shadow, yet we can't be certain. Suppose the man who became known as Thespis had decided that he had put up too long with speaking from cart tails (with little reward no doubt, and poor material) and had quit before the primitive theater evolved enough to interest Aeschylus? Western civilization could have existed without the theater, but it's hard for me to imagine it without what seems to me its central art. Thespis never knew what came of his decision to remain an actor. None of us ever knows what comes, finally, of his decisions. Usually not much. But whatever comes of them the essential problem is always the same. How do I relate my dream to the actual world, and how much of my dream will I sacrifice to make a portion of it come true?

The Politics of *Knickerbocker Holiday*

KNICKERBOCKER HOLIDAY WAS obviously written to make an occasion for Kurt Weill's music, and since Mr. Weill responded by writing the best score in the history of our theater, the venture would seem to justify itself without further comment.

But when the play came out there was a good deal of critical bewilderment over the political opinions expressed in it, and not a little resentment at my definitions of government and democracy. There might be less now because, among other things, Mr. Atkinson has visited Russia, and Mr. John Dos Passos has come round to seeing that there are no longer four freedoms but only one, the freedom from oppression. I have a notion that my definitions will not be shocking to anybody in the year 1947. They should not be, for they are only reminders of the attitude toward government that was current in this country at the time of the revolution of 1776 and throughout the early years of the Republic. At that time it was generally believed, as I believe now, that the gravest and most constant danger to a man's life, liberty, and happiness is the government under which he lives.

It was believed then, as I believe now, that a civilization is a balance of selfish interests, and that a government is necessary as an arbiter among these interests, but that the government must never be trusted, must be constantly watched, and must be drastically limited in its scope, because it, too, is a selfish interest and will automatically become a monopoly in crime and devour the civilization over which it presides unless there are definite and positive checks on its activities. The Constitution is a monument to our forefathers' distrust of the state, and the division of powers among the legislative, judicial, and executive branches has succeeded so well for more than a century in keeping the sovereign authority in its place, that our government is now widely regarded as a naturally wise and benevolent institution, capable of assuming the whole burden of social and economic justice.

The thinking behind our Constitution was dominated by such men as Franklin and Jefferson, men with a high regard for the rights of the individual, combined with a cold and realistic attitude toward the blessings of central authority. Knowing that government was a selfish interest, they treated it as such, and asked of it no more than a selfish interest can give.

But the coddled young reformer of our day, looking out on his world, finding merit often unrewarded and chicanery triumphant, throws prudence to the winds and grasps blindly at any weapon that seems to him likely to destroy the purse-proud haves and scatter their belongings among the deserving have-nots. Now he is right in believing that the accumulation of too much wealth and power in a few hands is a danger to his civilization and his liberty. But when the weapon he finds is a law, and when the law he enacts increases the power of the government over men's destinies, he is fighting a lesser tyranny by accepting a greater and more deadly one, and he should be aware of that fact.

A government is always, as Stuyvesant says in *Knickerbocker Holiday,* "a group of men organized to sell protection to the inhabitants of a limited area at monopolistic prices." The members of a government are not only in business, but in a business which is in continual danger of lapsing into pure gangsterism, pure terrorism and plundering, buttered over at the top by a hypocritical pretense at patriotic unselfishness. The continent of Europe was captured and temporarily held by such governments within the last few years, and our own government is rapidly assuming economic and social responsibilities that take us in the same direction. Whatever the motives behind a government-dominated economy, it can have but one result: a loss of individual liberty in thought, speech, and action. A guaranteed life is not free. Social security is a step toward the abrogation of the individual and his absorption into that robot which he has invented to serve him—the paternal state.

When I have said this to some of the youthful proponents of guaranteed existence I have been met with the argument that men must live, and that when the economic machinery breaks down, men must be cared for lest they starve or revolt. This is quite true and nobody opposes emergency relief. It is the attempt to make the emergency and the relief permanent that constitutes an attack on our free institutions. The greatest enemies of democracy, the most violent reactionaries, are those who have lost faith in the capacity of a free people to manage their own affairs and wish to set up the government as a political and social guardian, running their business and making their decisions for them.

For life is infinitely less important than freedom. A free man has a value to himself and perhaps to his time; a ward of the state is useless to himself—useful only as so many foot-pounds of energy serving those who manage to set themselves above him. A people which has lost its freedom might better be dead, for it has no importance in the scheme of things except as an evil power behind the word of a dictator. In our hearts we all despise the man who wishes the state to take care of him, who would not rather live meagerly as he pleases than suffer a fat and regimented existence. Those who are not willing to sacrifice their lives for their liberty have never been worth saving.

Throughout remembered time every self-respecting man has been willing to defend his liberty with his life. If our country goes totalitarian out of a soft-headed humanitarian impulse to make life easy for the many, we shall get what we vote for and what we deserve, for the choice is still before us, but we shall have betrayed the race of men, and among them the very have-nots whom we subsidize. Our western continent still has the opportunity to resist the government-led rush of barbarism which is taking Europe back toward Attila, but we can only do it by running our government, and by refusing to let it run us. If the millions of workingmen in this country who are patiently paying their social security dues could glimpse the bureaucratic absolutism which that act presages for themselves and their children, they would repudiate the whole monstrous and dishonest business overnight. When a government takes over a people's economic life it becomes absolute, and when it has become absolute it destroys the arts, the minds, the liberties, and the meaning of the people it governs. It is not an accident that Germany, the first paternalistic state in Europe, should have been taken over by an uncontrollable dictator; not an accident that Russia, adopting a centrally administered economy for humanitarian reasons, should arrive at a tyranny bloodier and more absolute than that of the Czars. Men who are fed by their government will soon be driven down to the status of slaves or cattle.

All this was known to the political leaders who put

our Constitution together after the revolution against England. The Constitution is so built that while we adhere to it we cannot be governed by one man or one faction, and when we have made mistakes we reserve the right to change our minds. The division of powers and the rotation of offices was designed to protect us against dictatorship and arbitrary authority. The fact that there are three branches of government makes for a salutary delay and a blessed inefficiency; the elective rotation makes for a government not by cynical professionals, but by normally honest and fairly incompetent amateurs. That was exactly what the wary old founding fathers wanted, and if we are wise we shall keep it, for no scheme in the history of the world has succeeded so well in maintaining the delicate balance between personal liberty and the minimum of authority which is necessary for the free growth of ideas in a tolerant society.

The Uses of Poetry

IN HIS ESTIMATE OF A SEASON'S POETIC PLAYS NOT so long ago, Max Eastman overpraised my playwriting most egregiously—and naturally I tried to forgive him. He also damned some of my versewriting for the theater most engagingly—and to that I had no answer. Nobody but an egomaniac can defend his own verse. But when Mr. Eastman stepped off the deep end and began to discuss the poetic drama in general, he revealed a confusion of mind so definite and so nearly typical of modern critics of the theater that I am tempted to point it out.

During the last quarter century, as he says, Mr. Eastman has been prophesying and hoping for an imaginative rebirth in this country which would include a re-establishment of the poetic theater. But the poetic theater he wants is a special kind of poetic theater, one which will throw its influence behind "the intelligent, which is to say the *practical scientific*—which is to say the *real*—effort to solve the problems of life on this planet."

The italics are Mr. Eastman's. And the italics leave no doubt that Mr. Eastman is asking not only for a new kind of poetic theater, but a new kind of poetry as well. Never in the history of the world has poetry of any excellence thrown its weight toward the practical or scientific reorganization of the affairs of men. Poetry is just as unfit for that business as for making up the accounts of a brokerage house. As for plays, even a play in prose loses its franchise over an audience the moment it begins to discuss the blueprints for an almost perfect state. Satire in verse and satire in prose are different matters. An attack on the existing order sometimes animates good poetry or a good play. But satire at its best is second or third best, and obviously Mr. Eastman was not asking for satire. He was not even asking for the burning anger at injustice which sometimes fires a poem or play. He was asking for something immediately constructive, scientifically and practically constructive.

He will never get it in poetry either on or off the stage, because a concrete constructive policy in the affairs of our planet has never yet called forth great poetry, and by its very nature cannot invoke great poetry, or any poetry at all. "Poetry is," as Mr. Eastman says, "a way of using language." But it is a way of using language that impels the user powerfully toward emotional utterance, impels him away from the small change of political economy and toward whatever vision he may be able to formulate of human destiny. The poetic impulse is a mystery that Mr. Eastman cannot explain any more than I can, but we can be certain of this about it—that it is no timeserver, that it cannot be hitched to the Marxian plow or turned on to campaign for a single tax. It is indulged in by dreamers and not by practical men, yet wherever the practical men have gone in search of truth or wealth they have found a few errant dreamers ahead of them. The poet is usually long dead by the time he inherits the earth, but he does inherit it.

The great poetry of Greece, of Italy, and of England is nearly all as mystic in concept and as prophetic in tone as the Old Testament itself. Prophetic with the eye on the distant horizon, not on the excavation in the foreground. Over and over again the poet, over-occupied with the horizon, steps, still singing, into the excavation for a new edifice, and is walled into the foundation quite unheeded. Over and over again his musical cry is remembered when the building is ruined or effaced; often there is little known of an entire civilization save the words of an obscure singer long ago buried under the fallen walls of a lost and forgotten political order.

And if we examine these musical cries for their meaning we find that the writers of epic, of lyric and dramatic verse are alike in having no pressing plans for the race. The writers of epics celebrate the youth, the hope, the victory, the disillusion, and the defeat of men; the writers of lyrics are always young, and their constant theme is the anguish of youth in its first contact with reality and inevitable despair; the authors of tragedy offer the largest hope for mankind which I can discern in the great poetry of the earth, a hope that man is greater than his clay, that the spirit of man may rise superior to physical defeat and death. The theme of tragedy has always been victory in defeat, a man's conquest of himself in the face of annihilation. The last act of a tragedy contains the moment when the wheel of a man's fate carries him simultaneously to spiritual realization and to the end of his life. The message of tragedy is simply that men are better than they think they are, and this message needs to be said over and over again in every tongue lest the race lose faith in itself entirely.

Perhaps Mr. Eastman thinks this message old-fashioned. Perhaps he still wants the Muses to divest themselves of whatever misty stuff they are wearing, don overalls, and go to work in the factory of the mind. But he has not said what practical and scientific plans for the advancement of the race he would set them to work on. I know of no such plans which would not be far more accurately discussed in cold prose in print than in verse on the stage. In fact, I know of no such plans which look further ahead for the race than the next few years, and none which appears so convincing in project or operation that a poet might be tempted to trail clouds of glory over it.

At this point Mr. Eastman, if he has been so far patient, may again call me a defeatist. But I am not a defeatist. My hope for the human race is that it will so far improve in mentality and magnanimity, over a period of millenniums, that it will be able to look back toward us, as we look back toward the great apes, and discern an improvement. It seems to me that it requires more steady courage to hold such a belief than to hide under the childish illusion that mankind will save itself by clever inventions, political, mechanical, or scientific. Socialism and communism are ingenious political inventions which would work if the majority of men were honest and unselfish, but they are not. They may be later on. My hope is that they will be. What savage disciplines, what devotion to the arts and sciences, what birth and death of races and race moralities must intervene between us and that far consummation, no man can guess or estimate. But when the race gets there, if it does, the poets will still be ahead of it, examining a still more distant future. For what the poets are always asking for, visioning, and projecting is man as he must and will be, man a step above and beyond his present, man as he may be glimpsed on some horizon of dream, a little nearer what he himself wishes to become.